Y0-CXL-693

DISCLAIMER: This is an **UNOFFICIAL** summary and study guide book. This book is not authorized, approved, licensed, or endorsed by the subject book's author or publisher. It is intended as a companion to, not a replacement for the original book.

Napoleon Hook is wholly responsible for this content and is not associated with the original author in any way.

TABLE OF CONTENTS

Introduction

The obesity epidemic has turned our world upside down but we cannot succeed in beating it. In **The Obesity Code**, Jason Fung sheds light on the history and causes behind the obesity problem that surrounds the United States. He also underlines the problem with conventional weight loss advice and why we cannot lose weight despite exercising so much. He further shares what we need to do to battle and avoid obesity.

Part 1: The Never Before Seen Prevalence of Obesity

1. What Caused Obesity to become an Epidemic?

The problem with conventional weight loss advice is that this advice is wrong. Conventional weight loss advice accentuates that people should eat less or drop their caloric intake to reduce weight. However, so many people are unable to reduce weight despite following this advice. Excessive calories might be the proximate cause behind weight gain but not the final cause.

Weight loss advice did not always use to be about calories. Till the 1950s, usual weight loss advice centered on reducing the consumption of refined carbohydrates or in other words, sugary and starchy substances.

Holding Fat Accountable Out of Nowhere

By the 1950s, people started considering heart disease an epidemic but this view was flawed. Vaccines, antibiotics and other health advancements increased the life expectancy of people by eliminating several fatal diseases. People now lived long enough to have heart attacks and there was no heart-related epidemic. Dietary fat was considered to be behind an increment in cholesterol, which was supposed to play a role in causing heart disease. Reducing the amount of dietary fat meant increasing the intake of proteins and carbohydrates in people's diet since these three offer the macronutrients required by the human body. Since proteins contain fat too, it ultimately meant increasing the intake of carbohydrates. Since most carbohydrates in the modern world are refined, this is the reason behind the obesity epidemic. Nutrition experts could not blame carbohydrates, so they started holding calories accountable for weight gain.

Criminalizing Fat

A governmental decree in 1977 blamed dietary fat for both heart disease and obesity. This played a part in defining the Dietary Goals for the U.S. These required eating a bigger number of carbohydrates and a lesser quantity of fats. Even calories were specified. Refined grains were now thought to be innocent. The American Heart Association recommended bread, pasta, and potatoes, which was problematic. The AHA even recommended carbonated soft drinks. Sugar consumption multiplied. Eating less fat and protein and more carbohydrates including sugar led to an increase in the obesity rates in 1977.

2. The Hereditary Nature of Obesity

The truth about obesity and its causes is actually different from the above. Obesity stays in families. Obese children usually turn into obese adults. Obese adults usually have obese children. Some genetic traits can lead to obesity but genes are not to be blamed completely for obesity. Families share an environment, and food patterns and approaches. Eating out, fast-food eateries, an increased amount of time in vehicles, more computer usage, and video games, more dietary sugar, bigger portion sizes and use of high-fructose corn syrup are all culprits behind the prevalence of obesity. Therefore, a majority of theories end up excluding genetic factors. However, genetic factors are among the most important factors in the context of obesity.

Genetic Factors versus the Environment

Adoptive families can shed light on this issue by a comparison between biological and adoptive parents of adoptees. A study in Denmark found a relation between the weight of adoptees with their biological parents and none with their adoptive parents. Another study indicated that our genes play a 70% part in our inclination to gain weight. But genetics is not the only factor since the obesity epidemic unfolded in a single generation.

The Thrifty-Gene Hypothesis

According to this hypothesis, which gained recognition in the 1970s, all humans are designed to gain weight as a survival system so that they can survive the scarcity of food. However, this gene is not ready for the excessive food availability of modern times and this causes obesity. This hypothesis is wrong because a thin animal would be more agile and have a better chance of surviving in a predatory world than a fat animal. Humans are not supposed to overeat because it makes them sick. Therefore, the hypothesis is incorrect.

Obesity refers to the degree of fatness that comes with harmful health effects. Evolution supported thinness instead of fatness. A baby's hormonal profile is defined by the setting in the womb, linked with high levels of insulin and leading to obesity in life afterward.

Part 2: The Issue with Calories

3. The Mistake Concerning Calorie Count

The main problem arises from the fact that obesity has been considered to stem from the way people treat calories. Obesity is seen as the difference between 'Calories In' and 'Calories Out'. The author calls it the calorie deception. Several myths exist regarding calories. Correcting the first wrong idea tells us that 'Calories In' and 'Calories Out' are quite dependent since lessening 'Calories In' also reduces 'Calories Out'. This means that if we restrict the number of calories we consume, we will also be limiting the amount of weight we can lose. The second important point accentuates that all calories are not identical when it comes to weight gain. Caloric intake from different foods can lead to unique metabolic and hormonal effects.

Further, it is assumed that exercise is the only factor that plays a role in calorie expenditure when it's not. Other functions also lead to energy expenditure. Eating excessively is not a conscious choice. Our hormones play a part in this choice as well.

Calorie reduction does not contribute principally to weight loss. Studies have discovered no link between calorie intake and weight gain. The human body has been designed to perform efficiently. When we decrease our caloric intake, it results in lessening our metabolic rate. In other words, this includes brain function, heart rate, body temperature, the growth of new tissues and other functions that need energy. Eating less leaves an effect on these and makes one sluggish. This further impedes weight loss. Even when a person stops having a lesser number of calories, the low metabolic rate continues. This leads to the caloric intake surpassing the caloric expenditure. The resulting imbalance leads to quick weight gain after trying to lose weight.

4. The Truth about Exercise

Exercise does not contribute majorly to weight loss. There is no denying the several benefits of exercise on our health but when it comes to weight loss, exercise does not play a huge role. Exercising does not decrease obesity because a lot of factors contribute to obesity. Obesity did not become an epidemic because physical activity decreased in our time. Our physical activity has actually increased from earlier. Also, our body's energy expenditure primarily originates from fundamental tasks such as breathing, sustaining core functions and body temperature, pumping blood, supporting the crucial organs, etc. rather than exercise. Other tasks such as moving around and performing basic chores also lead to energy expenditure.

5. The Riddle of Overeating

Eating too much or too less does not impact weight considerably in the long run. There is not much truth to overeating since the body cannot surpass a specific limit while eating. Furthermore, even when we overeat, our body boosts metabolism to get rid of the additional energy. Increased body heat can prove to be instrumental in expending approximately 70% of the excess energy. When we gain weight as a result of overeating, it is only a very small percentage of what the calorie hypothesis underlines. This weight does not persist. Similarly, when we lose weight by eating less, it does not stay off for a considerable amount of time. Our physiological sensors help our metabolism adapt and modify the body weight to reach its original point or body set weight. Those who experience obesity suffer because their original point is quite high.

We can pressurize our body weight to be greater than what our body wishes it to be for some time by having a greater number of calories. However, the consequential higher metabolism will lessen our weight to reach it normal value eventually. If we pressurize this body weight to reach a value lower than what our body wishes it to be by lessening the number of calories, the lowered metabolism will increase the weight in return eventually to its regular value.

A Hormonal Imbalance

A hormonal imbalance pertaining to the control of fat growth leads to obesity. Hormones regulate everything in our body including growth, blood sugar, etc. The hormones that regulate fat growth include leptin, adiponectin, and lipase, which play an instrumental role in obesity. Leptin is a protein that originates from fat cells and reaches the hypothalamus. The hypothalamus informs the body to boost or lessen hunger or metabolism to sustain fat stores at the defined point based on the leptin quantity that arrives. In case fat mass lessens, the levels of leptin decrease and the hypothalamus kindles appetite. In case of absence of food intake, it signals the body to lessen metabolism and restrict the amount of energy expenditure.

Therefore, based on leptin arrival, the hypothalamus controls the balance of energy and body weight. If the hypothalamus has faced harm, it can direct the body to gain weight in excess amounts, despite the individual being on a severe diet. Obesity results from leptin resistance instead of leptin shortage.

Part 3: Obesity: New Details and Definition

6. Insulin and Fat Amassing

The theory of obesity pertaining to the act of lessening calories to lose weight was half-baked and it did not help people lose weight and sustain it in the long run. The hormonal theory of obesity provides a clear answer. Insulin and cortisol play the most significant part in the context of weight gain. The intake of proteins, fats, and carbohydrates leads to the release of insulin in different quantities. It plays a role in deciding what happens to these food groups. Insulin opens cells to enable them to absorb glucose from our blood circulation and utilize it for energy. In case glucose levels decline, insulin informs cells to store part of the glucose to utilize later. When the glycogen in the liver runs out, insulin tells the cells to store the excess amount of glycogen in the form of fat for later use. Blood glucose quantities vary with the food group consumed. Refined carbohydrates increase blood sugar considerably as compared to protein and fats. This causes insulin release. Eating a lot and sustaining our glycogen storage takes the requirement to burn fat away from the body, which results in fat accumulation. High insulin levels cause the body to store fat and sugar, and low insulin levels cause it to burn fat and glycogen. Stable fasting and eating intervals cause the body not to lose or gain fat.

Obesity results from the hypothalamus commanding the body to boost the fat mass to go to the required body set weight. It changes the course of the available calories to boost fat, which causes the body to experience a lack of energy/calories. The body reacts by attempting to have more calories. It boosts the hormonal hunger signals and cuts the hormonal fullness signals. If we fight the impulse to have food and limit the number of calories we take, it will just confuse the hypothalamus for some time but it can go back to normal because of other things.

7. Insulin leads to Obesity

Insulin can make anyone fat over time, regardless of what they eat otherwise or how much they exercise. High levels of insulin are linked with higher body weights while low levels of insulin are linked with lower body weights. Increased insulin levels further boost fat storage and the body's set weight. The result in the set weight causes the hypothalamus to generate signals of appetite and hunger. When there is no food, the hypothalamus invokes the decreased metabolism to bring the body to the newly found set weight. Studies prove that injected insulin leads to weight gain. In addition, according to research, when insulin enters the body through some oral hypoglycemic agents or medications for type 2 diabetes, this leads to a boost in insulin levels as well. The sulfonylurea category of drugs causes the pancreas to give rise to an increased quantity of insulin to lessen blood sugar. While injected insulin boosts insulin levels considerably, sulfonylurea drugs also increase insulin levels but not as much as insulin itself. Metformin does not boost insulin levels. The sulfonylurea category of drugs also causes weight gain but not as much as insulin. Metformin does not lead to weight gain since it does not increase insulin levels in the body. Therefore, drugs that boost insulin levels can lead to a considerable amount of weight gain no matter how many calories a particular individual is taking. Insulin leads to maximum weight gain. Similarly, the drugs that leave a reducing impact on insulin levels can lead to weight loss. This is why type 1 diabetes causes extreme weight loss.

Thiazolidinedione drugs boost insulin sensitivity. Even though they do not boost the levels of insulin, they amplify its impact. They end up decreasing blood sugar but lead to weight gain since they boost the effect of insulin. Drugs that fall into the incretin agent category do not generally lead to weight gain. Even if they do, the weight gain is minimal. Some incretin agents with bigger doses can lead to weight loss. Alpha-glucosidase inhibitors lessen absorbed glucose and thus lower insulin levels slightly. This also causes a slight weight loss in patients. SGLT-2 inhibitors obstruct glucose reabsorption by the kidney so that it will go into the urine. This reduces the levels of blood sugar and the secretion of insulin. These inhibitors lessen glucose and insulin levels and ultimately cause weight loss in patients. They actually cause long-term weight loss. Other non-diabetic drugs can also leave an effect on weight gain and loss. In sum, an increase in insulin levels causes weight gain and a decrease in insulin levels causes weight loss.

8. Cortisol and Weight Gain

Other than insulin, another hormone related to weight gain is the stress hormone cortisol. Anyone can grow fat by consuming prednisone, which is the synthetic form of this hormone found in our body. Prednisone serves as the treatment of a number of diseases including cancer, rheumatoid arthritis, asthma, psoriasis, lupus, inflammatory bowel disease, myasthenia gravis, and glomerulonephritis. Prednisone leads to weight gain. Cortisol invokes the fight-or-flight system by limiting metabolic functions such as digestion, growth, and others for some time and transferring glycogen and glucose to muscles to offer energy so that an individual can either run or combat. While experiencing a threat, our body burns glucose while we run or fight. Chronic stress increases the body's glucose levels considerably since we do not exhaust ourselves to burn the available glucose. Cortisol leads to an increase in insulin levels by boosting glucose levels. Elevated insulin levels inspire fat accumulation and give rise to weight gain. When the gland that generates cortisol i.e. the adrenal gland experiences harm, it usually leads to weight loss. Sleep deprivation, which leads to chronic stress, stimulates cortisol and adds to the possibility of weight gain in many cases.

According to several studies, cortisol contributes to an increase in insulin resistance. Insulin resistance causes an increase in insulin levels. As mentioned above, insulin levels further play a crucial role in obesity.

9. The Atkins Diet: Not Effective on a Long-Term Basis

This brings us to the question of the foods that cause our insulin levels to escalate. The answer is refined carbohydrates i.e. sugars and extremely refined grains. Extremely refined carbohydrates are the main culprit behind an increase in blood sugar. Elevated blood sugar levels give rise to elevated insulin levels. Elevated insulin levels cause weight gain and eventually obesity. This refers to the carbohydrate-insulin hypothesis. An answer to this hypothesis was the diet suggested by Dr. Robert Atkins, which focused on a low carbohydrate plan. Even though the low-carb diet had been around before him, his book on the diet became extremely famous. According to recent research, the Atkins diet is more successful at lowering blood sugar and weight and favoring cholesterol and blood pressure than low-fat diets. The diet is successful, mostly on a short-term basis, since it lessens insulin levels, sustains metabolism and reduces hunger. However, it does not work on a long-term basis since after a year or so, those following this diet plan end up gaining weight since it is not easy to stick to the low-carb plan for a long time. Also, the proteins endorsed by the diet boost insulin levels, which increases weight. The diet does not consider the significance of fasting sufficiently.

The major problem with the Atkins diet becomes obvious here. The key factor that contributes to obesity is sugar instead of carbohydrates. In addition, whole and refined carbohydrates affect insulin levels differently. In Asian societies, white rice has been a part of the diet for decades but obesity is a new phenomenon. This strengthens the debate between refined and whole carbohydrates.

The notion that carbohydrates lead to weight gain because of insulin discharge is not completely baseless. Foods with high carbohydrate content add to insulin levels more than other macronutrients. Elevated insulin levels do give birth to obesity. The carbohydrate-insulin hypothesis is not wrong but it's not entirely complete. Other factors play a part in causing obesity as well and overall carbohydrate consumption does not cover everything in this context. Sugar plays more of a part in causing obesity than refined carbohydrates.

10. Insulin Resistance and its Harmful Effects

Long-term obesity is extremely hard to get rid of. Those who have experienced obesity for a long time cannot lose weight easily. Those who have gained weight of late can get rid of it much more easily. Insulin resistance is to be blamed for this since it operates in a diet independent and time-dependent manner. Timeframe plays a huge role in this context. High levels of insulin lead to obesity because of the phenomenon of insulin resistance.

When insulin cannot fit into the receptor, it means that the cell has become insulin resistant. This limits the quantity of glucose that can enter the cell. The cells become aware that the amount of glucose inside is quite less and the volume of glucose stocking outside the entrance is increasing. The cell requires more glucose since it is deprived of it. To make up for this, the body generates more insulin since it can help glucose enter the cell. This causes more pathways for glucose to open even though the fit is still not sufficient. Since resistance is present, our body has to produce more insulin to get normal glucose levels. This means that insulin resistance will keep the levels of insulin elevated.

Insulin resistance causes a further increase in insulin levels no matter what an individual consumes. Obesity keeps multiplying in this way. Insulin proves to be instrumental in opening the receptors that assist in letting glucose molecules enter cells. When the receptors experience high insulin levels reiteratively, it gives rise to insulin resistance. Therefore, what leads to insulin resistance in the first place is elevated insulin levels. The body attempts to shield itself with the assistance of insulin resistance. Extremely high insulin levels can lead to seizures or even death.

In case of low insulin levels or episodic surges, resistance does not develop. Time intervals between food intake and the food itself determine whether we will experience insulin resistance or not. When we take three meals a day with proper time intervals, this stabilizes a small time period of insulin surges with many hours of low insulin levels. Snacking between meals causes the body to go through continuously high insulin levels.

Part 4: The Social Aspect of Obesity

11. Changes in Food Consumption, Obesity, and Diabetes

Snacking is Harmful

We have been fooled to believe that snacking is good for us. This is a lie and just utilized to trick us into purchasing commercially produced snacks. Even nutritionists and other seemingly trustworthy names that promote snacking do it because they are set to enjoy some form of benefits from this endorsement. When we incorporate ready-to-use snacks in our diet, this increases the likelihood of replacing healthy food with unhealthy items. Snacking further decreases the gap between our meals and keeps our insulin levels constantly high. We must avoid snacking between meals to lower our insulin levels.

Breakfast Can be Skipped

Breakfast is not necessary at all. We do not need breakfast and even if we eat a lot for breakfast, it will not keep us full or cause us to eat less during the day. A heavy breakfast will not give rise to weight loss. Our body automatically produces a sufficient quantity of glucose to provide energy after waking up and keep us going. Breakfast further does not affect our energy.

12. The Connection between Poverty and Obesity

In the United States, poor people are more obese. This gives rise to a dilemma because rich people whose work does not require a lot of movement should be more obese. In addition, the rich have more food at their disposal. Yet the states whose populations are poor demonstrate a prevalence of obesity.

Highly refined carbohydrates explain obesity in poor regions of the United States. One of the major factors that have contributed to obesity among the poor includes governmental policies that endorse the industry of refined carbohydrates and their usage. The poor cannot afford proteins since they are more expensive. Dietary fats do not attract people as much as carbohydrates since they are not as tasty. This leaves the poor with refined carbohydrates, which are cheap and found in abundance. The government's biggest subsidies lie in foods such as wheat, corn, etc. and additives including soy oils and corn syrup. These subsidies support the production of such foods in huge quantities, reduce their cost and boost their intake. The rest is evident from the patterns of food consumption.

13. The Childhood Facet of Obesity

Obesity in infants has left experts perplexed. What explains this efficiently is the surplus in insulin levels. A mother's high insulin levels end up being transferred to the fetus. This causes the fetus to go through hormonal imbalances as well. High insulin levels further cause the fetus to experience insulin resistance. Obesity in a mother increases the probability of her infant being obese. In addition, an obese child experiences more of a probability of being an obese adult than other children. The fact that such small children are experiencing obesity is alarming.

Part 5: The Issue with Our Diet

14. How Fructose Contributes to Obesity

Even though the nature of sugar has been established as harmful, another sweet flavor that became accepted all around was fructose. Food firms shifted their attention to fructose in their products. Sugary drinks have been part of our diet for decades now. This pattern has a close link with the epidemic of obesity. When we take fructose in the form of high-fructose corn syrup in several processed foods including sauces, ketchup and bread, and drinks containing sugar, this can lead to weight gain and even type 2 diabetes in several cases.

Fructose works differently from glucose and can only be processed by the liver. This means that fructose cannot be utilized for energy. The accumulation of some form of fructose in liver cells can harm the function of the liver and give birth to insulin resistance. In other words, fructose does not get metabolized. The effects of fructose in this context, as evident from studies, are severe. Fructose has played an instrumental role in the obesity epidemic.

15. The Facts about Diet Soda

It is evident that we need to get rid of drinks and foods that have fructose. This includes any juices and teas that have sugar, sodas and all forms of soft drinks. However, the alternative i.e. artificial sweeteners are just as bad. Even though these sweeteners seem to be favorable to our bodies on the surface since they offer a lesser number of calories, they do not lessen weight in any form. The problem arises from the detail that despite having no sugar, these sweeteners do boost insulin levels. Therefore, they also add to the probability of obesity. If an individual consumes two or more diet sodas on a daily basis, it increases the likelihood of heart attacks and strokes.

16. Which Carbohydrates Contribute to Weight Gain and Which Do Not?

The bad reputation of carbohydrates commenced with their role in obesity. The glycemic index sheds light on the degree to which specific food items add to the levels of blood glucose in the form of a value. Proteins and fats do not impact blood glucose considerably and are not part of the index for this reason. Naturally occurring carbohydrates such as brown rice, boiled potatoes etc. have a low glycemic index while processed carbohydrates such as cornflakes, white bread, etc. have a high glycemic index.

When wheat and corn get transformed into their processed forms, the highly concentrated products end up having a high value of the glycemic index.

What happens to Dietary Fiber?

The problem with processed foods is that processing leads to the elimination of the food parts that restrict insulin levels. In other words, processing eliminates dietary fibers, proteins, and fats to make food last longer and enhance its taste. This further leaves a negative effect on the natural levels of stabilization that monitor the levels of insulin. Fiber refers to that component of carbohydrates that cannot be easily digested, gives a full feeling to our tummy, and lessens food consumption. Fiber proves to be instrumental in lessening insulin levels and blood glucose by lessening the concentration of carbohydrates. When plant foods have not gone through the phenomenon of processing, they contain fiber. These details clarify the reason why people in earlier times consumed a lot of natural foods containing carbohydrates but did not experience obesity in considerable numbers.

17. Proteins and Insulin Levels

Different food groups incite the release of insulin in their own manner. The elimination of carbohydrates from diet plans resulted in the addition of proteins and fats. Even this resulted in the release of insulin. The glycemic index can trick those who are trying to lose weight because it only takes those foods into account that boost blood glucose but excludes those that add to insulin levels. Even when there is no glucose, insulin levels can increase. In addition, blood glucose only contributes to a quarter of the amount of insulin that unfolds. The insulin index calculates the quantity of the boost of insulin levels as a result of consumed food. Therefore, the insulin index is better at shedding light on how foods impact weight. This applies to proteins and fats.

When we consume food, the body prepares itself for it and despite the food category, the insulin levels end up getting increased. This means that any type of food can lead to weight gain. As far as proteins and fats are concerned, they are responsible for 10% of insulin discharge in the body. The cause behind approximately 70% of insulin discharge is unidentified.

Therefore, the ultimate food category that is entirely bad is processed food, regardless of whether it is proteins, fats or carbohydrates. We should stick to natural foods and avoid processed ones as much as possible if we want to stay healthy and fit.

18. Dietary Fat is Not Bad

Fats were held responsible for leaving a negative effect on our cardiovascular system decades ago. Our body is full of cholesterol. The liver is responsible for generating 80 % of our blood cholesterol to utilize it to form the membranes that offer the outer layer of cells. Even though earlier studies linked high blood cholesterol levels with heart disease, this theory was debunked later since they did not have any proper evidence to support the idea. Research conducted later demonstrated that consuming saturated fats does not lead to a boost in blood cholesterol or give rise to heart disease.

When some nutritionists endorse a diet with low fat, they generalize various fats and do not acknowledge the difference in the properties of specific foods. Even though artificial trans fats including margarine add to the levels of bad cholesterol, lessen the levels of good cholesterol and boost the possibility of heart disease, natural saturated fats including butter actually lessen the possibility of heart attack. When we combine dietary fats such as whole milk, sour cream, cheese, etc. with other food items, they decrease the surges of glucose and insulin in our body.

Part 6: How to Solve the Problem with Our Diet

19. Foods we Should Consume to Reduce Weight

An incomplete diet cannot respond properly to the problem of obesity. If a diet does not consider what illnesses originate from, it will not succeed in helping us. Our body requires a cautious blend of nutrients that will not release as much insulin as a flawed diet. Most diets achieve weight loss but they only work temporarily. Success stops in a year or a half and people return to a condition of weight gain even though they are still following the dietary rules that helped them reduce weight in the first place. Diets are usually successful in the start since they respond to a few variables that lead to weight gain and make the hypothalamus lessen the set weight of the body. However, when the set weight decreases, the body battles to go back to the condition it considers to be stable.

A proper weight plan that works on lessening weight and then sustaining the condition of weight loss must focus on the cause behind the elevated levels of insulin. Several factors prove to be instrumental in giving rise to obesity. These include carbohydrates, sugars, calories, fats, proteins, etc. A lack of sleep also plays a part. Therefore, a weight loss plan that only responds to a couple of these factors and does not take the rest into account fails in the long run.

A proper plan to respond to obesity should commence with evaluating the hormonal imbalance that is causing it. If our body is experiencing high insulin levels because of excess carbohydrates or sugar, we need to eliminate these foods from our diet considerably. If the cause behind elevated insulin levels is a lack of sleep, we need to get a sufficient amount of sleep first.

Action Plan

Firstly, get rid of sugar from both drinks and foods.

Secondly, bid goodbye to artificial sweeteners as well.

The third step should be to reduce the consumption of processed foods as much as possible since an overwhelming majority of these foods have sugars added to them. Food labels including sucrose, glucose, fructose, maltose, nectar and corn sweetener all refer to sugar.

We also need to lessen the use of sauces and condiments including ketchup since they have sugar in huge quantities as well.

We further need to avoid sweet drinks such as fruit juices, vitamin water, energy drinks, smoothies, etc. (Red wine is acceptable in moderate quantities).

We need to substitute desserts including candy, ice cream, cakes, etc. with fresh fruits, cheeses, nuts or dark chocolate in reasonable quantities.

We need to eliminate snacks from our diets to balance our insulin levels. Snacking leads to a continual spike in insulin levels since a majority of snacks have elevated quantities of refined sugar and flour. This can cause the development of insulin resistance. Green tea is an effective snack substitute.

We can skip breakfast if we do not feel hungry. Our body does not actually feel hunger in the morning and water, coffee or tea can suffice. We can start eating at noon. Even when we have breakfast, we can go for whole foods including eggs instead of instant oatmeal, bakery items, and sugary breakfast cereals to avoid refined sugars and carbohydrates.

We further need to lessen our intake of refined grains including white flour. They lack nutrients and contribute to insulin release comparatively more than other items. Therefore, we need to lessen our intake of pasta, white flour, noodles, and bakery items to achieve proper weight loss by restricting insulin surges.

To consume dietary fiber and shield against insulin spikes, we need to consume whole grains and other forms of unprocessed carbohydrates.

We further need to eat proteins in reasonable amounts and have more natural fats. Only 20 to 30% of our overall calories should be proteins. Dietary fats are better when it comes to insulin stimulation than proteins and carbs.

Take unprocessed fats including butter, virgin olive oil, and coconut oil since they have benefits because of their anti-inflammatory and antioxidant properties. They lessen the possibility of cardiovascular disease and lower cholesterol levels.

Avoid extremely processed vegetable oils, which also include 'pure olive oil' since it can play a part in causing heart disease. Full-fat dairy leaves weight unchanged.

Consume fiber-rich foods in more quantities to regulate insulin and weight gain. Dietary fiber in natural whole foods can be extremely helpful.

Take vinegar since it curbs insulin surges as well.

20. The Timing of Food and the Importance of Intermittent Fasting

The intervals of time between our food consumption play an instrumental role in defining our body weight as well. Without proper regulation of these intervals, we may not be able to achieve weight loss despite doing everything right when it comes to food consumption. If we frequently take meals, it will lead to an increase in the levels of insulin and lead to a rise in weight gain. Insulin resistance stems from elevated levels of insulin. The only way to balance this is to replicate time intervals of extremely low levels of insulin. Therefore, while proper eating stops insulin surges from happening, the only way to lessen insulin levels is fasting. Intermittent fasts of 24 to 36 hours really help.

Fasting is an ancient healing method that has been proven to improve people's health. It is recommended in several mainstream religions as well. Once an individual is a day into a fast, it gives rise to glucose depletion. Insulin levels also decline. The body starts processing the glycogen storage in the liver to offer energy. Between 24 to 72 hours, fat gets split into fatty acids to offer energy to sustain tissues. The body holds the capability to deal with a temporary lack of food. A fast further entails a boost in overall energy expenditure. Adrenaline also gets amplified to sustain the levels of energy. In simple words, intermittent fasting can work wonders in the context of losing weight and staying healthy.

Conclusion

We cannot deny the obesity epidemic. Whether we are obese or not, we need to be extremely careful about what we eat since our world is full of processed foods and refined carbohydrates that are extremely harmful to us. In this book, Jason Fung asks us to watch what we eat. He further suggests that we find the root cause if we are obese and respond to it. To lose weight, we should stop focusing on calories and restrict the number of refined carbohydrates and sugars. In addition to eating healthy, we also need to utilize intermittent fasting to keep our weight in check. If we follow the advice in this book, we can embark on our path to a healthy existence.

Appendix from the Book

EXAMPLE MEAL PLAN: 7 DAYS

These are just suggestions. Avoid snacking entirely.

24-Hour Fasting

Sample 7-Day Meal Plan – 24-hour Fasting Protocol

	Monday	Tuesday	Wednesday	Thursday	Friday	Saturday	Sunday
Breakfast	FAST DAY Water Coffee	Western Omelette Green apple	FAST DAY Water Coffee	All-Bran Buds with milk Mixed berries	FAST DAY Water Coffee	Two eggs Breakfast sausage/bacon Strawberries	FAST DAY Water Coffee
Lunch	FAST DAY Water Green tea 1 cup of vegetable broth	Arugula salad with walnuts, slices of pear, goat cheese	FAST DAY Water Green tea 1 cup of chicken broth	Ginger chicken lettuce cups Stir-fried vegetables	FAST DAY Water Green tea 1 cup of beef broth	Baby spinach and lentil salad	FAST DAY Water Green tea 1 cup of vegetable broth
Dinner	Herbed chicken Green beans Mixed berries for desert	Asian grilled pork belly Baby bok choy stir-fry No desert	Halibut pan-fried in butter and coconut oil No desert	Indian chicken curry Cauliflower Green salad No desert	Baked catfish Sautéed broccoli with garlic and olive oil Seasonal fruits for desert	Peppered steak Asparagus	Grilled chicken salad Dark chocolate for desert

36-Hour Fasting

Sample 7-Day Meal Plan – 36-hour Fasting Protocol

	Monday	Tuesday	Wednesday	Thursday	Friday	Saturday	Sunday
Breakfast	FAST DAY Water Coffee	Western Omelette Green apple	FAST DAY Water Coffee	All-Bran Buds with milk Mixed berries	FAST DAY Water Coffee	Two eggs Breakfast sausage/bacon Strawberries	FAST DAY Water Coffee
Lunch	FAST DAY Water Green tea 1 cup of vegetable broth	Arugula salad with walnuts, slices of pear, goat cheese	FAST DAY Water Green tea 1 cup of chicken broth	Ginger chicken lettuce cups Stir-fried vegetables	FAST DAY Water Green tea 1 cup of beef broth	Baby spinach and lentil salad	FAST DAY Water Green tea 1 cup of vegetable broth
Dinner	FAST DAY Water Green Tea + No desert	Asian grilled pork belly Baby bok choy stir-fry + no desert	FAST DAY Water Green Tea + No desert	Indian chicken curry Cauliflower Green salad + no desert	FAST DAY Water Green tea + Seasonal fruits	Peppered steak Asparagus + No desert	FAST DAY Water Green tea + No desert

Made in the USA
Middletown, DE
21 May 2019